LOST FOREVER

EXTINCT
ANIMALS OF THE
NORTHERN CONTINENTS

Barbara J. Behm and Jean-Christophe Balouet

Gareth Stevens Publishing
MILWAUKEE

For a free color catalog describing Gareth Stevens' list of high-quality books and multimedia programs, call 1-800-542-2595 (USA) or 1-800-461-9120 (Canada).
Gareth Stevens Publishing's Fax: (414) 225-0377.
See our catalog, too, on the World Wide Web: http://gsinc.com

The editor would like to extend special thanks to Jan W. Rafert, Curator of Primates and Small Mammals, Milwaukee County Zoo, Milwaukee, Wisconsin, for his kind and professional help with the information in this book.

Library of Congress Cataloging-in-Publication Data available upon request from publisher. Fax (414) 225-0377 for the attention of the Publishing Records Department.

ISBN 0-8368-1526-2

This North American edition first published in 1997 by
Gareth Stevens Publishing
1555 North RiverCenter Drive, Suite 201
Milwaukee, Wisconsin 53212, USA

This edition © 1997 by Gareth Stevens, Inc. Based on the book *Extinct Species of the World,* © 1990 by David Bateman, Ltd. (English Language Edition) and © 1989 by Editions Ouest-France (French Language Edition), with original text by Jean-Christophe Balouet and illustrations by Eric Alibert. This edition published by arrangement with David Bateman, Ltd. Additional end matter © 1997 by Gareth Stevens, Inc.

Picture Credits
Eric Alibert: Cover, pp. 6, 7, 9, 10, 12, 13 (bottom), 15, 19, 22 (both), 24, 25, 26, 27; J. C. Balouet: p. 18; Jacana: p. 13 (top); R. Landin: p. 11; Larousse: title, p. 21; National Library: p. 23; © Science VU/Visuals Unlimited: p. 28; D. Serrette, Institute of Paleontology, National Museum of Natural History: p. 5; D. Serrette, Mammals, National Museum of Natural History: p. 17

Series editor: Patricia Lantier-Sampon
Series designer: Karen Knutson
Additional picture research: Diane Laska
Map art: Donna Genzmer Schenström, University of Wisconsin-Milwaukee Cartographic Services Laboratory
Series logo artwork: Tom Redman

Printed in the United States of America

1 2 3 4 5 6 7 8 9 01 00 99 98 97

For millions of years, during the course of evolution, hundreds of plant and animal species have appeared on Earth, multiplied, and then, for a variety of reasons, vanished. We all know of animals today — such as the elephant and the rhinoceros, the mountain gorilla and the orangutan — that face extinction because of irresponsible human activity or changes in environmental conditions. Amazingly, hundreds of species of insects and plants become extinct before we can even classify them. Fortunately, in modern times, we are beginning to understand that all living things are connected. When we destroy a plant species, we may be depriving the world of an amazing cure for human diseases. And we know that if we destroy the forest, the desert creeps forward and the climate changes, wild animals die off because they cannot survive the harsh conditions, and humans, too, face starvation and death. Let us remember that every creature and plant is part of a web of life, each perfect, each contributing to the whole. It is up to each of us to end the destruction of our natural world before it becomes too late. Future generations will find it hard to forgive us if we fail to act. No matter what our age or where we live, it is time for every one of us to get involved.

Dr. Jane Goodall, Ethologist

CONTENTS

Words that appear in the glossary are printed in **boldface** type the first time they occur in the text.

NORTHERN CONTINENTS

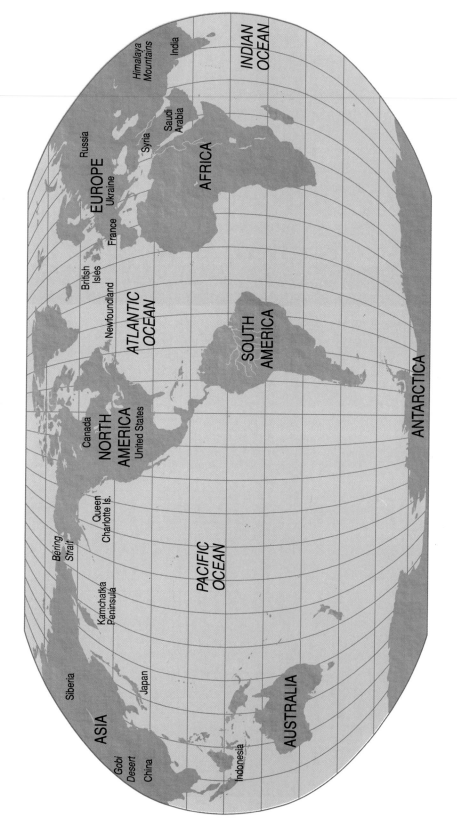

ASIA

EUROPE

Russia

Ukraine

France

British Isles

Newfoundland

Himalaya Mountains

India

INDIAN OCEAN

Syria

Saudi Arabia

AFRICA

ATLANTIC OCEAN

SOUTH AMERICA

ANTARCTICA

NORTH AMERICA

Canada

United States

Queen Charlotte Is.

Bering Strait

Kamchatka Peninsula

PACIFIC OCEAN

Siberia

Japan

AUSTRALIA

Gobi Desert

China

Indonesia

▲ Many species of plant and animal life on Earth have become extinct, and many more species are in imminent danger. This tragic situation is not limited to any one place; it is a global problem. From the northern and southern continents to the islands of Earth's oceans and seas, numerous animal species have disappeared forever. Only the intervention of human resources may now be able to save currently **endangered** animals. This map indicates some of the continents, countries, bodies of water, and other areas referred to in *Lost Forever: Extinct Animals of the Northern Continents*.

A DELICATE BALANCE

The earliest human settlement in Europe was in France. Two-million-year-old tools used by humans were found alongside the remains of a mastodon. This indicates that early humans probably hunted the massive mastodon for food.

The environment has changed greatly since the first human settlement. The many **ice ages** that have occurred have each brought about extensive changes in **flora** and **fauna**.

The actions of humans have also caused disturbances in wildlife. Unfortunately, these actions have led to a number of **extinctions**.

BIRDS

A crane, *Grus primigenia*, may have been hunted into extinction by humans. Climatic changes may also explain its disappearance.

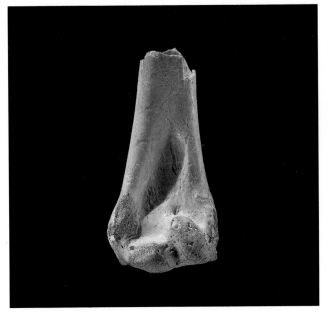

▲ The crane, *Grus primigenia*, is known only from its limb bones.

MAMMALS

The mammoth, *Mammuthus primigenius*, was hunted by humans throughout Europe and other continents except South America and Australia. This gigantic animal stood over 13 feet (4 meters) tall — about the same size as a modern elephant. Many mammoths had a woolly undercoat about 1 inch (2.5 centimeters) thick. This undercoat lay beneath a coarse coat of dark hair and helped insulate the animal in harsh weather. Humans found other uses for the mammoth besides food. The tusks were carved into statuettes. The bones and tusks were then arranged in a circle so that each supported the other. This structure was then covered with skins to provide shelter.

The aurochs, *Bos primigenius*, was a primitive ox depicted in cave paintings by early humans. This ox stood more than 6.5 feet (2 m) tall and had spiral horns that could reach a length of 32 inches (81 cm). Humans hunted the aurochs for food, carved its bones into tools, and shaped

▲ The European mammoth, *Mammuthus primigenius*, was hunted for its meat, tusks, and bones. This specimen was exhibited in St. Petersburg, Florida, in 1804.

▲ The aurochs, *Bos primigenius*, shown in an ancient cave painting, became extinct by 1627.

its skin into clothing. It was extinct by 1627. The European bison, *Bison bonasus*, often confused with the aurochs, is very rare today. Only the Polish **subspecies** has managed to survive.

The Caucasian subspecies, *Bison bonasus caucasicus*, has disappeared. In 1805, there were about four hundred left, but these numbers dwindled due to hunting. In 1915, there were one hundred left, and protective measures were

▲ Although *Bison priscus* may have been plentiful at one time, it eventually disappeared because our ancestors hunted it.

undertaken, including the establishment of a **reserve**. But some people were unhappy about being moved from their land to create the reserve. They took revenge by killing the animals. In 1921, the bison numbered only 50. Just 15-20 were left in 1923. The last known representative of the **species** died in 1925.

The extinct cave bear, *Ursus spelaeus*, was probably a peaceful animal. Like most bears, it **hibernated** for many months of the year. It may have fallen victim to human interference because its bones were often used in religious rituals performed by humans.

The Pyrenean ibex, once very numerous, included at least

two subspecies. **Cross-breeds** of *Capra pyrenaica pyrenaica* may still exist somewhere. *Capra pyrenaica lusitanica* is thought to have disappeared in 1892. Its body was similar to that of a goat, but the horns of this ibex

▲ The cave bear, *Ursus spelaeus*, was a peaceful vegetarian.

▲ The subspecies of the Pyrenean ibex, *Capra pyrenaica lusitanica*, was intensively hunted into extinction by humans.

could reach more than 3 feet (1 m) long.

The Irish elk, *Megaloceros giganteus*, a giant species of deer, had huge antlers. These antlers, which were greater in size than any other known deer, measured as much as 13 feet (4 m) across. The Irish elk's **habitat** extended over most of Europe, but its last refuge was in the north of England and Ireland. It was probably extinct by 700 B.C. or 500 B.C. The antlers of the males grew too big and heavy for survival. Fossils, found mainly in peat bogs, date from the Pleistocene Era — 2,500,000 to 10,000 years ago.

▲ The enormous antlers of the extinct Irish elk, *Megaloceros giganteus*, could reach more than 13 feet (4 m) across.

MOST POPULOUS

Asia is the largest of all the world's continents. It is also the world's most populous continent, by far. Human intervention has caused a strain on some of the native wildlife and has contributed to extinctions.

For example, rhinoceroses have been hunted in Asia for centuries for their horns. Poachers make money by selling the horns for use as a so-called **aphrodisiac**, particularly in China.

The Asian lion, *Panthera leo persicus*, inhabited the Near and Middle East until the beginning of the nineteenth century. It is now found only on the Kathiawar Peninsula in India. Due to hunting by humans, fewer than two hundred animals survive.

Przewalski horses, *Equus przewalskii*, now exist only in zoos. The Asiatic wild asses of India, *Equus hemionus khur*, are at risk of the same fate.

Ironically, the giant panda, *Ailuropoda melanoleuca*, the world symbol for nature preservation, appears condemned to become extinct in spite of efforts made to protect it.

▲ A painting of an antelope hunt in Iran.

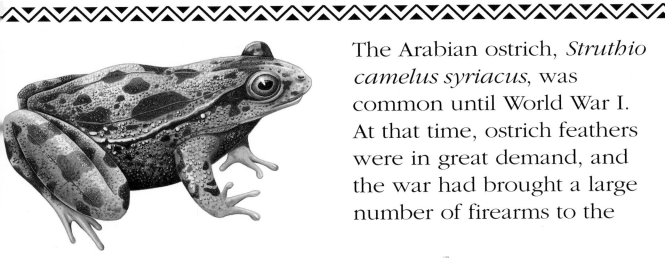

▲ The Palestinian painted frog, *Discoglossus nigriventer*, is known only from five specimens, two of them tadpoles. They all died in a laboratory while under study.

AMPHIBIANS

The Palestinian painted frog, *Discoglossus nigriventer*, once inhabited Lake Hula on the Israeli-Syrian border. It was not discovered until 1940, and it disappeared in 1956. The painted frog was a victim of the destruction of its wetland home.

BIRDS

Blewitt's owl, *Athene blewitti*, of central India survived until 1914. It became extinct due to the destruction of its forest home.

The Arabian ostrich, *Struthio camelus syriacus*, was common until World War I. At that time, ostrich feathers were in great demand, and the war had brought a large number of firearms to the

▲ Blewitt's owl, *Athene blewitti*, disappeared after the destruction of its forest habitat.

13

▲ The pink-headed duck, *Rhodonessa caryophyllacea*, was sold as an ornamental bird. It never reproduced in captivity and died out completely in 1935.

area. The end came for this ostrich during World War II. The last member of the species was eaten by a German tank crew in 1944.

The Chinese ostrich, *Struthio asiaticus*, is known only from eggshell fragments. The last ostrich of this species was eaten at an imperial meal during the Third Dynasty.

The pink-headed duck, *Rhodonessa caryophyllacea*, was discovered at the end of the eighteenth century. It lived in the lower basins of

the Ganges and Brahmaputra rivers in India. It measured about 2 feet (60 cm) long and became extinct in 1935. It was lost because of the drainage and destruction of its wetland home.

The Himalayan mountain quail, *Ophrysia superciliosa*, lived at an altitude of 5,000-7,500 feet (1,500-2,300 m). It was the highest-dwelling of any of the extinct birds. It was last observed in 1868.

▲ The Himalayan mountain quail, *Ophrysia superciliosa*, lived at the highest altitude of any known extinct bird.

MAMMALS

The Japanese wolf, *Canis lupus hodophylax*, was called *shamanu* by the Japanese. It was the smallest species of wolf ever known, measuring just over 3 feet (1 m) long. The Japanese hunted the shamanu because they feared it and because its skin brought a high price. The last known shamanu was killed in Japan in 1920.

The Bali tiger, *Panthera tigris balica*, was the smallest of the tigers. It is the only sub-species of tiger to have died out so far, although all tigers are seriously endangered in the wild today. The Bali tiger

▲ The *shamanu*, or Japanese wolf, *Canis lupus hodophylax*, was the smallest wolf ever known.

population was abundant at the beginning of the twentieth century, but it became endangered by 1935. It was continually hunted, however, and the last one was killed by firearms in 1937.

The black bear, *Ursus arctos piscator*, lived until the beginning of the twentieth century on the Kamchatka Peninsula in Russia. This bear, which weighed up to 1,500 pounds (680 kilograms), was hunted into extinction by 1920.

Schomburgk's deer, *Cervus schomburgki*, lived in Thailand. This deer was hunted mainly for the velvet on its antlers, to which the Chinese attributed many medicinal qualities. The deer lived in marshes, moving from island to island, and hunters harpooned it from boats. In addition, the draining of the marshes and

▲ The Bali tiger, *Panthera tigris balica*, is the only subspecies of tiger to have completely disappeared. However, the other subspecies are all seriously endangered today.

the cultivation of the land caused this deer to become extremely rare. The introduction of firearms led to its final destruction.

Two Asian species of Equidae are extinct. The tarpan, *Equus ferus gmelini*, was a pony in eastern Europe and Asia. It also roamed the Ukrainian and Mongolian steppes and the Gobi Desert. It was used as a working animal by

trappers and mammoth ivory hunters in Siberia. The last known wild tarpan was killed in Russia in 1879. The last in captivity died in 1887.

Equus hemionus hemippus of Syria was a small ass about 3 feet (1 m) tall. It lived in Syria, Palestine, Arabia, and ancient Mesopotamia. Because of its size and wild nature, the Syrian *hemippus* was not successfully domes-

▲ The wild ass from Syria, *Equus hemionus hemippus*, was the smallest, boldest, and swiftest of the asses. It became extinct in 1928.

ticated. Instead, it was hunted for its meat. The introduction during World War I of firearms and moving vehicles that could chase animals on the run sealed the fate of this species. The last wild specimen was killed in 1927 while drinking water at an oasis. The last specimen of *Equus hemionus hemippus* in captivity died in 1928.

Many animals in Asia today are almost extinct, such as the tiger, *Panthera tigris*; the Java rhinoceros, *Rhinoceros sondaicus*; the snow leopard, *Panthera uncia*; and the orangutan, *Pongo pygmaeus*.

AN ENDANGERED PEOPLE

North America was settled more than thirty thousand years ago by American Indians who crossed the Bering Strait on an ice bridge. This giant continent covers an area of more than 7.3 million square miles (19 million square kilometers).

There were several million American Indians living in North America in 1700. But soon afterward, due to the arrival of European settlers who brought new weapons and diseases with them, the American Indian population dropped drastically. By 1920, there were fewer than a

▲ American Indians dried fish and game over an open fire.

quarter of a million Indians left. The entire Beothuk tribe of Newfoundland became extinct due to the actions of European settlers.

FISH

North America has lost seventeen species and subspecies of freshwater fish.

▲ The hare-lipped suckerfish, *Lagochilla lacera*, became extinct in 1893.

The fat-tailed dace, *Gila crassicauda*, lived in calm waters and stagnant waterholes in California. It grew to a length of 1 foot (30 cm) and was the favorite fish of the American Indians. Drainage of the dace's habitat caused it to become extinct in 1945.

The hare-lipped suckerfish, *Lagochilla lacera*, swam in the basins of the Ohio and Mississippi rivers. Its lower lip was almost divided into two. This allowed it to graze on the algae growing on rocky river bottoms. With **deforestation** came soil **erosion**. This caused a discharge of mud into the hare-lipped suckerfish's habitat. The algae on which the fish fed died out, and the fish themselves were choked by the clay-laden water. The last hare-lipped suckerfish was caught in 1893.

The snub-nosed suckerfish, *Chasmistes brevirostris*, lived in Lake Klamathy in Oregon. It reproduced in contaminated rivers until it died out in 1960.

Two species of cisco, *Coregonus nigripennus* and *Coregonus johannae*, lived in Lake Huron and Lake Michigan. They were heavily overfished with nets. Fifteen million tons were caught in 1885 alone. **Predator** fish called lampreys were also introduced into the Great Lakes, completing the elimination of these two cisco species in 1960.

BIRDS

The Labrador duck, *Camptorhynchus labradorius*, frequented the east coast from New Brunswick to Chesapeake Bay during winter. It died out about 1875.

The painted vulture, *Sarcorhamphus sacra*, was the size of a turkey. It became extinct in the nineteenth century.

▲ The Labrador duck, *Camptorhynchus labradorius*, became extinct in approximately 1875.

▲ The last seaside sparrow died in 1987.

of these pigeons died in a zoo in 1914.

The heath hen, *Tympanuchus cupido cupido*, lived on the plains of Massachusetts and the Carolinas. Legal measures to protect the bird were undertaken as early as 1791 when experts realized the hen was rare. Destruction of

The last seaside sparrow, *Ammospiza maritima*, died in its cage at Disney World park in Florida in 1987.

The passenger pigeon, *Ectopistes migratorius*, once numbered in the hundreds of millions. American Indians hunted the pigeon for food for thousands of years. But upon the arrival of Europeans, the passenger pigeon was hunted into extinction. The last wild specimen was sighted in 1899. The very last

▲ Hundreds of millions of passenger pigeons were slaughtered in the nineteenth century. This bird became extinct in 1914.

▲ The last Carolina parrot, *Conuropsis carolinensis*, survived in a zoo until 1914.

grasslands, introduced predators, and hunting led to the hen's demise. The bird disappeared from the continent by 1870 and survived on only a few islands. A reserve was set up in 1915 with 20,000 birds, but poachers killed them. The last heath hens lived on the island of Martha's Vineyard in Massachusetts until 1932.

The last Carolina parrot, *Conuropsis carolinensis*, died in 1914 in a zoo, the same year the last passenger pigeon died. Some farmers claimed that the Carolina parrots were harmful to crops, so the birds were purposely destroyed. Hunters also killed the parrots for food. Disease may also have played a part in the parrots' extinction.

MAMMALS

Long before Europeans arrived, several species of large mammals had already disappeared. Examples include the North American mastodon, *Mastodon americanum*; the giant beaver, *Casteroides*; the western camel, *Camelops hesternus*; and a giant jaguar, *Panthera atrox*.

In later times, the American bison, *Bison bison*, became the basic resource of the American Indian economy and industry. The Indians ate bison meat, and they used the skins for clothing and roofing; the bones for tools, knives, needles, hooks, and toys; and the horns and hooves for "kitchen" utensils.

▲ The North American mastodon was hunted by American Indians for its meat and skin.

▲ The giant beaver, *Casteroides*, was more than 6 feet (2 m) long. It was extinct before the arrival of Europeans.

When Europeans arrived, the American bison population was about 75 million. The U.S. Army soon began to kill the bison. They did this because one way to destroy the population of American Indians was to destroy what the Indians depended upon.

Of the four American bison subspecies, two survive today. The eastern bison, *Bison bison pennsylvanicus*, and the Oregon bison, *Bison bison oreganus*, have died out.

The Queen Charlotte Islands caribou, *Rangifer tarandus*

dawsoni, inhabited Queen Charlotte Island in British Columbia. Europeans offered the Haida Indians who lived there a reward for every caribou skin they could present, and the killing began. The last Queen Charlotte Islands caribou died in 1908.

Eight North American subspecies of wolves are extinct because of intensive hunting and poisoning. From 1850 to 1900, two million wolves were killed in this manner by humans.

The lobo, *Canis lupus nubilus*, disappeared in 1926 after being the most common wolf in North America. It lived in Manitoba, Canada, and in southern Texas.

▲ Two of the four subspecies of bison have disappeared from North America. Shown is the extinct eastern, or Pennsylvanian, bison, *Bison bison pennsylvanicus*.

▲ The Queen Charlotte Islands caribou, *Rangifer tarandus dawsoni*, was prized for its skin.

Many other North American animals are now extinct. These include the Mexican grizzly, *Ursus arctos nelsoni*; a subspecies of jaguar, *Felis onca veracrucensis*; the Canadian elk, *Cervus canadensis canadensis*; the Badlands (or Audubon's) bighorn sheep, *Ovis canadensis auduboni*; and the sea mink, *Mustela macrodon*.

BREAKING THE CYCLE

Every effort is needed to see that today's endangered plant and animal species do not follow in the tragic footsteps of the species that have already become extinct.

27

Many nations have passed important legislation to protect wildlife and the environment. The United Nations formed the IUCN — now known as the World Conservation Union — in 1948. The United States passed the Endangered Species Act in 1973. This legislation is designed to protect wildlife as well as their habitats. Many private organizations have also been created to help with wildlife and habitat conservation.

It is up to each of us to get actively involved in conservation activities. By working together to save all the other species in the great web of life, we also save ourselves.

▲ Many wolf species were once common in North America's vast landscape.

SCIENTIFIC NAMES OF THE ANIMALS IN THIS BOOK

Animals have different names in every language. To simplify matters, researchers the world over have agreed to use the same scientific names, usually from ancient Greek or Latin, to identify animals. With this in mind, most animals are classified by two names. One is the genus name; the other is the name of the species to which they belong. Additional names indicate further subgroupings. The scientific names for the animals included in *Lost Forever: Extinct Animals of the Northern Continents* are:

American bison . . . . *Bison bison*
Arabian ostrich . . . . *Struthio camelus syriacus*
Asian lion . . . . *Panthera leo persicus*
Asiatic wild ass . . . .*Equus hemionus khur*
Aurochs . . . . *Bos primigenius*
Badlands (Audubon's) bighorn sheep . . . .
. . . . *Ovis canadensis auduboni*
Bali tiger . . . . *Panthera tigris balica*
Black bear . . . . *Ursus arctos piscator*
Blewitt's owl . . . . *Athene blewitti*
Canadian elk . . . . . *Cervus canadensis canadensis*
Carolina parrot . . . . *Conuropsis carolinensis*
Caucasian bison . . . . . *Bison bonasus caucasicus*
Cave bear . . . . *Ursus spelaeus*
Chinese ostrich . . . . *Struthio asiaticus*
Cisco (2 species) . . . . *Coregonus johannae*
. . . . *Coregonus nigripennus*
Crane . . . . *Grus primigenia*
Eastern bison . . . . . . *Bison bison pennsylvanicus*
European bison . . . . *Bison bonasus*
Fat-tailed dace . . . . *Gila crassicauda*
Giant beaver . . . .*Casteroides*
Giant jaguar . . . .*Panthera atrox*
Giant panda . . . . . . *Ailuropoda melanoleuca*
Hare-lipped suckerfish . . . . *Lagochila lacera*
Heath hen . . . . *Tympanuchus cupido cupido*
Himalayan mountain quail . . . .
. . . . *Ophrysia superciliosa*
Irish elk . . . . *Megaloceros giganteus*
Japanese wolf . . . . *Canis lupus hodophylax*

Java rhinoceros . . . . *Rhinoceros sondaicus*
Labrador duck . . . . *Camptorhynchus labradorius*
Lobo . . . . *Canis lupus nubilus*
Mammoth . . . . *Mammuthus primigenius*
Mexican grizzly . . . . . . *Ursus arctos nelsoni*
North American jaguar . . . .
. . . . *Felis onca veracrucensis*
North American mastodon . . . .
. . . . *Mastodon americanum*
Orangutan . . . . *Pongo pygmaeus*
Oregon bison . . . . *Bison bison oreganus*
Painted vulture . . . .*Sarcorhamphus sacra*
Palestinian painted frog . . *Discoglossus nigriventer*
Passenger pigeon . . . . . . *Ectopistes migratorius*
Pink-headed duck . . . *Rhodonessa caryophyllacea*
Przewalski horse . . . .*Equus przewalskii*
Pyrenean ibex . . . . . . *Capra pyrenaica pyrenaica*
. . . . *Capra pyrenaica lusitanica*
Queen Charlotte Islands caribou . . . .
. . . . *Rangifer tarandus dawsoni*
Schomburgk's deer . . . . *Cervus schomburgki*
Sea mink . . . .*Mustela macrodon*
Seaside sparrow . . . .*Ammospiza maritima*
Snow leopard . . . . *Panthera uncia*
Snub-nosed suckerfish . . . *Chasmistes brevirostris*
Syrian wild ass . . . . . . *Equus hemionus hemippus*
Tarpan . . . . *Equus ferus gmelini*
Tiger . . . .*Panthera tigris*
Western camel . . . . *Camelops hesternus*

GLOSSARY

aphrodisiac — a substance that is believed to contain elements that will increase sexual potency.

crossbreed — a plant or animal that is the result of the mating of two different species or subspecies.

deforestation — the cutting down or clearing out of trees in a forest.

endangered — in peril or danger of dying out completely, or becoming extinct. Asia's giant panda is an endangered species.

erosion — the process in which an object is slowly eaten away by the elements.

extinction — the dying out of all members of a plant or animal species.

fauna — a region's animal life.

flora — a region's plant life.

habitat — an environment in which plants and animals live and grow.

hibernation — a state of rest or inactivity in which most bodily functions, such as heartbeat and breathing, slow down.

ice ages — periods of time when glaciers were widespread on Earth.

predators — animals that eat other animals for food.

reserve — an area of land set aside for the protection of animal and plant species.

species — a group of animals that share the same physical characteristics.

subspecies — a further subdivision of the larger species category.

MORE BOOKS TO READ

Endangered! (series). Bob Burton (Gareth Stevens)

Extinct Animals of the World. Clive Roots (Sterling)

The Extinct Species Collection (series). (Gareth Stevens)

Extinction: The Causes and Consequences of the Disappearance of Species. Paul R. and Anne H. Ehrlich (Random House)

In Peril (series). Barbara J. Behm and J-C Balouet (Gareth Stevens)

VIDEOS

Alaskan Safari. (United Home Video)

The Grizzlies. (National Geographic)

Vanishing Wilderness. (Pacific International)

WEB SITES

http://envirolink.org/

http://netvet.wustl.edu/wildlife.htm

PLACES TO WRITE

The following organizations educate people about animals, promote the protection of animals, and encourage the conservation of natural habitat. Include a self-addressed, stamped envelope for a reply.

International Wildlife
    Coalition
70 East Falmouth Highway
East Falmouth, MA 02536

Canadian Wildlife
    Federation
2740 Queensview Drive
Ottawa, Ontario K2B 1A2

World Wildlife Fund
1250 24th Street, N.W.
Washington, D.C. 20037

Greenpeace
1436 U Street, N.W.
Washington, D.C. 20009

Canadian Nature
    Federation
One Nicholas Street
Suite 520
Ottawa, Ontario K1N 7B7

Royal Society for the
    Prevention of Cruelty
    to Animals
3 Burwood Highway
Burwood East
Victoria 3151 Australia

International Fund for
    Animal Welfare
P.O. Box 2587
Rivonia 2128, South Africa

International Fund for
    Animal Welfare
P.O. Box 56
Paddington, New South
    Wales 2021
Australia

Department of
    Conservation
P.O. Box 10-420
Wellington, New Zealand

National Wildlife
    Federation
8925 Leesburg Pike
Vienna, VA 22184

ACTIVITIES TO HELP SAVE ENDANGERED SPECIES

1. Write the United States Department of the Interior, Publications Unit, Fish and Wildlife Service, Washington, D.C., 20240, for a list of endangered wildlife. Then write to government officials and express your support for the protection of these animals and their habitat.

2. Write to government officials to express your support of strengthening the Endangered Species Act.

3. Do not buy wild or exotic animals as pets. Also, do not buy fur, bearskin rugs, ivory, or any other products that endanger animals.

4. If you become aware of the sale of ivory or any other illegal trade in animals or animal products or the use of illegal pesticides, contact your local authorities.

5. Contact a wildlife rehabilitation center in your area and find out what educational programs or activities they are offering to the public.

INDEX